JUN - - 2010

Jesus Blesses the Children

MARK 10: 13-16

AND they brought young children to him, that he should touch them: and his disciples rebuked those that brought them.

14 But when Jesus saw it, he was much displeased, and said unto them, "Suffer the little children to come unto me, and forbid them not: for of such is the kingdom of God.

15 Verily I say unto you, Whosoever shall not receive the kingdom of God as a little child, he shall not enter therein."

16 And he took them up in his arms, put his hands upon them, and blessed them.

The First and Greatest Commandment

LUKE 10: 27

AND he answering said, "Thou shalt love the Lord thy God with all thy heart, and with all thy soul, and with all thy strength, and with all thy mind; and thy neighbor as thyself."

The Golden Rule

MATTHEW 7:12

"THEREFORE all things whatsoever you would that men should do to you, do you even so to them: for this is the law and the prophets."

art by

GENNADY SPIRIN

JESUS

HIS LIFE IN VERSES

from the

KING JAMES HOLY BIBLE

MARSHALL CAVENDISH CHILDREN

Marshall Cavendish Corporation, 99 White Plains Road, Tarrytown, NY 10591

www.marshallcavendish.us/kids

LIBRARY OF CONGRESS CATALOGING-IN-PUBLICATION DATA

Spirin, Gennadii.

Jesus / illustrated by Gennady Spirin. — 1st ed. p. cm.

ISBN 978-0-7614-5630-8

1. Jesus Christ—Biography—Sources, Biblical—Juvenile literature. I. Title.

BT299.3.S66 2010   232.9'01—dc22   2009005956

The artrwork is rendered in tempera.

Book design by Michael Nelson

Editor: Margery Cuyler

Printed in China (E)

First edition

1 3 5 6 4 2

For His Holiness Patriarch Kirill
of Moscow and All Russia
—G. S.

A Note about the Painting

The tempera painting on which this book is based is 40″ x 49″. Each fragment of the painting is a stand-alone illustration in the book. The designer, Michael Nelson, isolated and digitally reproduced the fragments to illustrate the Biblical passages.

The composition presents architectural space with various levels of receding perspective. The painting is of a Biblical city with arcade-like windows, inviting the reader to explore the most important stages of Jesus Christ's life. It combines both stylized and realistic features and iconic symbolism typical of the early Renaissance artists.

The Annunciation

LUKE I: 26-38

$\mathcal{A}$ND in the sixth month the angel Gabriel was sent from God unto a city of Galilee, named Nazareth,

27 To a virgin espoused to a man whose name was Joseph, of the house of David; and the virgin's name was Mary.

28 And the angel came in unto her, and said, "Hail, thou that art highly favored, the Lord is with thee: blessed art thou among women."

29 And when she saw him, she was troubled at his saying, and cast in her mind what manner of salutation this should be.

30 And the angel said unto her, "Fear not, Mary: for thou hast found favor with God.

31 And, behold, thou shalt conceive in thy womb, and bring forth a son, and shalt call his name JESUS.

32 He shall be great, and shall be called the Son of the Highest, and the Lord God shall give unto him the throne of his father David:

33 And he shall reign over the house of Jacob forever; and of his kingdom there shall be no end."

34 Then said Mary unto the angel, "How shall this be, seeing I know not a man?"

35 And the angel answered and said unto her, "The Holy Ghost shall come upon thee, and the power of the Highest shall overshadow thee: therefore also that holy thing which shall be born of thee shall be called the Son of God.

36 And, behold, thy cousin Elizabeth, she hath also conceived a son in her old age: and this is the sixth month with her, who was called barren.

37 For with God nothing shall be impossible."

38 And Mary said, "Behold the handmaid of the Lord; be it unto me according to thy word." And the angel departed from her.

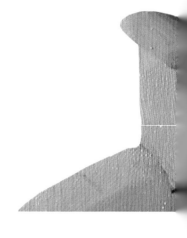

The Birth

AND it came to pass in those days, that there went out a decree from Caesar Augustus, that all the world should be taxed.

2 (And this taxing was first made when Cyrenius was governor of Syria.)

3 And all went to be taxed, every one into his own city.

4 And Joseph also went up from Galilee, out of the city of Nazareth, into Judaea, unto the city of David, which is called Bethlehem (because he was of the house and lineage of David),

5 To be taxed with Mary his espoused wife, being great with child.

6 And so it was, that, while they were there, the days were accomplished that she should be delivered.

7 And she brought forth her firstborn son, and wrapped him in swaddling clothes, and laid him in a manger, because there was no room for them in the inn.

The Baptism

MATTHEW 3: 13-17

*T*HEN cometh Jesus from Galilee to Jordan unto John, to be baptized of him.

14 But John forbade him, saying, "I have need to be baptized of thee, and comest thou to me?"

15 And Jesus answering said unto him, "Suffer it to be so now: for thus it becometh us to fulfill all righteousness." Then he suffered him.

16 And Jesus, when he was baptized, went up straightway out of the water: and, lo, the heavens were opened unto him, and he saw the Spirit of God descending like a dove, and lighting upon him:

17 And lo a voice from heaven, saying, "This is my beloved Son, in whom I am well pleased."

The Boy Jesus in the Temple

LUKE 2: 41-52

*N*OW his parents went to Jerusalem every year at the feast of the Passover.

42 And when he was twelve years old, they went up to Jerusalem after the custom of the feast.

43 And when they had fulfilled the days, as they returned, the child Jesus tarried behind in Jerusalem; and Joseph and his mother knew not of it.

44 But they, supposing him to have been in the company, went a day's journey; and they sought him among their kinsfolk and acquaintance.

45 And when they found him not, they turned back again to Jerusalem, seeking him.

46 And it came to pass, that after three days, they found him in the temple, sitting in the midst of the doctors, both hearing them, and asking them questions.

47 And all that heard him were astonished at his understanding and answers.

48 And when they saw him, they were amazed: and his mother said unto him, "Son, why hast thou thus dealt with us? Behold, thy father and I have sought thee sorrowing."

49 And he said unto them, "How is it that ye sought me? Know ye not that I must be about my Father's business?"

50 And they understood not the saying which he spoke unto them.

51 And he went down with them, and came to Nazareth, and was subject unto them: but his mother kept all these sayings in her heart.

52 And Jesus increased in wisdom and stature, and in favor with God and man.

The Fast and Temptation of Jesus

MATTHEW 4: 1-11

$\mathcal{T}$HEN was Jesus led up of the Spirit into the wilderness to be tempted of the devil.

2 And when he had fasted forty days and forty nights, he was afterward hungry.

3 And when the tempter came to him, he said, "If thou be the Son of God, command that these stones be made bread."

4 But he answered and said, "It is written, Man shall not live by bread alone, but by every word that proceedeth out of the mouth of God."

5 Then the devil taketh him up into the holy city, and setteth him on a pinnacle of the temple,

6 And saith unto him, "If thou be the Son of God, cast thyself down: for it is written, He shall give his angels charge concerning thee: and in their hands they shall bear thee up, lest at any time thou dash thy foot against a stone."

7 Jesus said unto him, "It is written again, Thou shalt not tempt the Lord thy God."

8 Again, the devil taketh him up into an exceeding high mountain, and sheweth him all the kingdoms of the world, and the glory of them;

9 And saith unto him, "All these things will I give thee, if thou wilt fall down and worship me."

10 Then saith Jesus unto him, "Get thee hence, Satan: for it is written, Thou shalt worship the Lord thy God, and him only shalt thou serve."

11 Then the devil leaveth him, and, behold, angels came and ministered unto him.

The Marriage in Cana

JOHN 2: 1-11

AND the third day there was a marriage in Cana of Galilee; and the mother of Jesus was there:

2 And both Jesus was called, and his disciples, to the marriage.

3 And when they wanted wine, the mother of Jesus saith unto him, "They have no wine."

4 Jesus saith unto her, "Woman, what have I to do with thee? Mine hour is not yet come."

5 His mother saith unto the servants, "Whatsoever he saith unto you, do it."

6 And there were set there six water pots of stone, after the manner of the purifying of the Jews, containing two or three firkins apiece.

7 Jesus saith unto them, "Fill the water pots with water." And they filled them up to the brim.

8 And he saith unto them, "Draw out now, and bear unto the governor of the feast." And they bare it.

9 When the ruler of the feast had tasted the water that was made wine, and knew not whence it was: (but the servants which drew the water knew;) the governor of the feast called the bridegroom,

10 And saith unto him, "Every man at the beginning doth set forth good wine; and when men have well drunk, then that which is worse: but thou hast kept the good wine until now."

11 This beginning of miracles did Jesus in Cana of Galilee, and manifested forth his glory; and his disciples believed on him.

The Sermon on the Mount (The Beatitudes)

MATTHEW 5: 1-12

𝒜ND seeing the multitudes, he went up into a mountain: and when he was set, his disciples came unto him:

2 And he opened his mouth, and taught them, saying,

3 "Blessed are the poor in spirit: for theirs is the kingdom of heaven.

4 Blessed are they that mourn: for they shall be comforted.

5 Blessed are the meek: for they shall inherit the earth.

6 Blessed are they which do hunger and thirst after righteousness: for they shall be filled.

7 Blessed are the merciful: for they shall obtain mercy.

8 Blessed are the pure in heart: for they shall see God.

9 Blessed are the peacemakers: for they shall be called the children of God.

10 Blessed are they which are persecuted for righteousness' sake: for theirs is the kingdom of heaven.

11 Blessed are ye, when men shall revile you, and persecute you, and shall say all manner of evil against you falsely, for my sake.

12 Rejoice, and be exceeding glad: for great is your reward in heaven: for so persecuted they the prophets which were before you."

The Transfiguration

MARK 9: 1-8

AND he said unto them, "Verily I say unto you, That there be some of them that stand here, which shall not taste of death, till they have seen the kingdom of God come with power."

2 And after six days Jesus taketh with him Peter, and James, and John, and leadeth them up into an high mountain apart by themselves: and he was transfigured before them.

3 And his raiment became shining, exceeding white as snow; so as no fuller on earth can white them.

4 And there appeared unto them Elijah with Moses: and they were talking with Jesus.

5 And Peter answered and said to Jesus, "Master, it is good for us to be here: and let us make three tabernacles; one for thee, and one for Moses, and one for Elijah."

6 For he knew not what to say; for they were sore afraid.

7 And there was a cloud that overshadowed them: and a voice came out of the cloud, saying, "This is my beloved Son: hear him."

8 And suddenly, when they had looked round about, they saw no man any more, save Jesus only with themselves.

The Raising of Lazarus at Bethany

JOHN 11: 32-44

THEN when Mary was come where Jesus was, and saw him, she fell down at his feet, saying unto him, "Lord, if thou hadst been here, my brother had not died."

33 When Jesus therefore saw her weeping, and the Jews also weeping which came with her, he groaned in the spirit, and was troubled,

34 And said, "Where have ye laid him?" They said unto him, "Lord, come and see."

35 Jesus wept.

36 Then said the Jews, "Behold how he loved him!"

37 And some of them said, "Could not this man, which opened the eyes of the blind, have caused that even this man should not have died?"

38 Jesus therefore again groaning in himself cometh to the grave. It was a cave, and a stone lay upon it.

39 Jesus said, "Take ye away the stone." Martha, the sister of him that was dead, saith unto him, "Lord, by this time he stinketh: for he hath been dead four days."

40 Jesus saith unto her, "Said I not unto thee, that, if thou wouldest believe, thou shouldest see the glory of God?"

41 Then they took away the stone from the place where the dead was laid. And Jesus lifted up his eyes, and said, "Father, I thank thee that thou hast heard me.

42 And I knew that thou hearest me always: but because of the people which stand by I said it, that they may believe that thou hast sent me."

43 And when he thus had spoken, he cried with a loud voice, "Lazarus, come forth."

44 And he that was dead came forth, bound hand and foot with grave clothes: and his face was bound about with a napkin. Jesus saith unto them, "Loose him, and let him go."

The Last Supper
MATTHEW 26:20-29

*N*OW when the even was come, he sat down with the twelve.

21 And as they did eat, he said, "Verily I say unto you, that one of you shall betray me."

22 And they were exceeding sorrowful, and began every one of them to say unto him, "Lord, is it I?"

23 And he answered and said, "He that dippeth his hand with me in the dish, the same shall betray me.

24 The Son of man goeth as it is written of him: but woe unto that man by whom the Son of man is betrayed! It had been good for that man if he had not been born."

25 Then Judas, which betrayed him, answered and said, "Master, is it I?" He said unto him, "Thou hast said."

26 And as they were eating, Jesus took bread, and blessed it, and brake it, and gave it to the disciples, and said, "Take, eat; this is my body."

27 And he took the cup, and gave thanks, and gave it to them, saying, "Drink ye all of it;

28 For this is my blood of the new testament, which is shed for many for the remission of sins.

29 But I say unto you, 'I will not drink henceforth of this fruit of the vine, until that day when I drink it new with you in my Father's kingdom.'"

The Crucifixion

AND they bring him unto the place Golgotha, which is, being interpreted, The place of a skull.

23 And they gave him to drink wine mingled with myrrh: but he received it not.

24 And when they had crucified him, they parted his garments, casting lots upon them, what every man should take.

25 And it was the third hour, and they crucified him.

26 And the superscription of his accusation was written over, THE KING OF THE JEWS.

27 And with him they crucify two thieves; the one on his right hand, and the other on his left.

28 And the scripture was fulfilled, which saith, "And he was numbered with the transgressors."

29 And they that passed by railed on him, wagging their heads, and saying, "Ah, thou that destroyest the temple, and buildest it in three days,

30 Save thyself, and come down from the cross."

31 Likewise also the chief priests mocking said among themselves with the scribes, "He saved others; himself he cannot save.

32 Let Christ the King of Israel descend now from the cross, that we may see and believe." And they that were crucified with him reviled him.

33 And when the sixth hour was come, there was darkness over the whole land until the ninth hour.

34 And at the ninth hour Jesus cried with a loud voice, saying, "Eloi, Eloi, lama sabachthani?" which is, being interpreted, "My God, my God, why hast thou forsaken me?"

35 And some of them that stood by, when they heard it, said, "Behold, he calleth Elijah."

36 And one ran and filled a sponge full of vinegar, and put it on a reed, and gave him to drink, saying, "Let alone; let us see whether Elijah will come to take him down."

37 And Jesus cried with a loud voice, and gave up the ghost.

The Resurrection

MATTHEW 28: 1-8

*I*N the end of the sabbath, as it began to dawn toward the first day of the week, came Mary Magdalene and the other Mary to see the sepulcher.

2 And, behold, there was a great earthquake: for the angel of the Lord descended from heaven, and came and rolled back the stone from the door, and sat upon it.

3 His countenance was like lightning, and his raiment white as snow:

4 And for fear of him the keepers did shake, and became as dead men.

5 And the angel answered and said unto the women, "Fear not ye: for I know that ye seek Jesus, which was crucified.

6 He is not here: for he is risen, as he said. Come, see the place where the Lord lay.

7 And go quickly, and tell his disciples that he is risen from the dead; and, behold, he goeth before you into Galilee; there shall ye see him: lo, I have told you."

8 And they departed quickly from the sepulcher with fear and great joy; and did run to bring his disciples word.

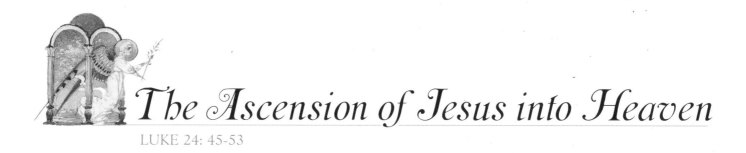

The Ascension of Jesus into Heaven

THEN opened he their understanding, that they might understand the scriptures,

46 And said unto them, "Thus it is written, and thus it behooved Christ to suffer, and to rise from the dead the third day:

47 And that repentance and remission of sins should be preached in his name among all nations, beginning at Jerusalem.

48 And ye are witnesses of these things.

49 And, behold, I send the promise of my Father upon you: but tarry ye in the city of Jerusalem, until ye be endued with power from on high."

50 And he led them out as far as to Bethany, and he lifted up his hands, and blessed them.

51 And it came to pass, while he blessed them, he was parted from them, and carried up into heaven.

52 And they worshipped him, and returned to Jerusalem with great joy:

53 And were continually in the temple, praising and blessing God. Amen.